125
£5

J. M. Russell.

BRING BACK THE BELLS

By the same Author

"WELL, ANYHOW . . ." OR, LITTLE TALKS
LET US BE GLUM
SIREN SONG
GENERAL CARGO
SIP! SWALLOW!
THE "AYES" HAVE IT
MILD AND BITTER
WHAT A WORD!
HOLY DEADLOCK
THE WATER GIPSIES
UNCOMMON LAW
MISLEADING CASES IN THE COMMON LAW
MORE MISLEADING CASES
STILL MORE MISLEADING CASES
MR. PEWTER
"NO BOATS ON THE RIVER"
HONEYBUBBLE & CO.
THE SECRET BATTLE
THE HOUSE BY THE RIVER
THE OLD FLAME
TANTIVY TOWERS
DERBY DAY
HELEN
THE BOMBER GIPSY, AND OTHER POEMS
THE WHEREFORE AND THE WHY
"TINKER, TAILOR . . ."
WISDOM FOR THE WISE
TOPSY, M.P.
THE TRIALS OF TOPSY
LAUGHING ANN
SHE-SHANTIES
PLAIN JANE
BALLADS FOR BROADBROWS

BRING BACK THE BELLS

by

A. P. HERBERT

METHUEN & CO., LTD., LONDON
36 Essex Street, Strand, W.C.2

First published in 1943

Seven of these pieces appeared originally in *Punch*, the remainder in the *Sunday Graphic*. My thanks to the proprietors of both papers for permitting me to print them again.

THIS BOOK IS PRODUCED IN COMPLETE CONFORMITY
WITH THE AUTHORIZED ECONOMY
STANDARDS

*Printed in Great Britain
by The Camelot Press Limited, London and Southampton*

CONTENTS

RED BREAD

(With Compliments and Congratulations to the First Baron Woolton)

I NEVER, NEVER liked brown bread,
Whatever aunts and uncles said.
In vain they tried to make me see
This beastly food was good for me.
Though full of nourishment (said Nurse)
It looked like mud, and tasted worse;
And I would seldom care a lot
If things were good for me, or not.
(Yes, even at that early age
Foul Self-indulgence took the stage,
And I would tend to sulk, or strike,
If barred from what I chanced to like.)
At all events, I laid it down:
The bread I ate should *not* be brown.

Years passed; and other people sought
To make me eat as Britons ought.
"Brown bread" was pressed on me no more;
The "whole-meal loaf" became the bore.
And though I liked the novel name
The stuff, I thought, was much the same.
Men saw me pleasantly engrossed
In bread-and-cheese or buttered toast,
And wondered how a man could eat
"De-naturized" anæmic wheat.
They said, for all the goodness there
One might as well consume a chair,
Fry bits of blotting-pad, or hat,
Or spread one's butter on the mat.
I answered, "Nature was not meant
To be a one-stringed instrument.

7

She plays for each a different tune,
E.g." (I said) "observe the moon
And how the tide is high elsewhere
When it's Low Water over there."

I said that since the age of two
White bread had been the bread I knew,
And that, as far as I could see,
Was what was "natural" for me.
At all events, I laid it down
That bread I ate should *not* be brown.

But now, through Hitler and his works,
We find ourselves in other circs.
The Government, I understand,
Of our superb but sea-girt land
Are starting, just to win the war,
This prehistoric hare once more;
And they desire us all to eat
This unattractive whole-meal wheat.
Well, more than anything, I love
To do the will of H.M. Gov.
I don't like Communists much more
Than, right or wrong, I did before.
But as I now salute the Red
So will I bow to dear brown bread
Because, as my wise rulers say,
We shall save tonnage in this way
(They tell me half a million tons
Will thus be wrested from the Huns).
But let this point be understood—
No man must tell me it is *good*:
Nor shall I jump with girlish glee
If someone screams it's good for *me*.

My principles shall not be shed:
I say, *I do not like brown bread!*
I will attempt this awful thing
To save the sailors of the King;
I contemplate some loss of face
That we may have more cargo-space.
And you, I'm sure, for very shame
Will ultimately do the same.

But when we've put the Prussian down,
The bread I eat will *not* be brown.

July 23, 1941

LAMENT FOR A LORD

(To H. S.—that was)

WEEP, MR. SPEAKER, weep (if it's in order),
For one of us has crossed the fatal border,
Taken the steps no mortal can retrace,
Gone down the passage to another place.
Chairman of Ways and Means, there's news to tell;
Serjeant-at-Arms, awake, and weep as well.
Weep, all you Whips (if men so stern are able),
Weep, all you Clerks assembled at the Table,
For our dear —— has become a lord;
And, oh, my goodness—oh, he will be bored!

You will be lost in that expanse of red
Where much is done but not so much is said.
Not that you talk a lot, or ever sought
To cross the boundaries of Should and Ought—
But there is this about the H. of C.,
It's not so dull as it appears to be.
Though all seems calm and placid as a cow,
At any moment there may be a row.
The slow debate crawls drowsily along
Till some young Minister puts one foot wrong;
And Members laugh, and interrupt, and shout,
The Speaker rises, and the Whips rush out,
And while the Cabinet in comfort dine
The legislators cry, "Resign! Resign!"
To-morrow all is quiet as a mouse—
But that's the merit of the Commons House.

Now, in that other place, austere, serene,
A revolution could not cause a scene.

Though the mad mob surged in with shot and shell,
And parachutists on the Woolsack fell,
I doubt—and I may add that I rejoice—
If any noble lord would raise his voice.
Before the tumbrils were allowed to fill
The House would pass the Widnes (Drainage) Bill.
But while we praise, with patriotic airs,
The artful chemistry of our affairs,
By which we mix in one immense retort
Two elements so separate in sort—
Like the two parts of certain drugs, it's said,
One the blue powder and the other red,
The change is hard, conceal it how you can,
On one who was "a House of Commons man".

And such were you. But now no more, no more
May you be seen on our exclusive floor—
Though we may spot you, laughing through our tears,
In that high cranny where we put the peers.
But to the Smoking-room we still admit
The sad lost souls who from our body flit.
There shall you find us, when for us you yearn,
As Old Boys wistfully to school return.
There will we gossip, as we used to do,
And finish Hitler with a word or two;
There will we give the Government some tips,
And say exactly what we think of Whips.
Yes, there shall be a candle at the door
To light you back when lords become a bore,
And by the candle, welcoming you in,
A large dry sherry or a small pink gin.

August 6, 1941

HONOUR THE OLD

HONOUR THE OLD, the patient and the brave.
  To gallant youth all proper praise be sung,
Who open life at war on wing or wave:
  Yet I am not so sorry for the young . . .

The old who face the darkness and the noise,
  The shops, the queues, the traffic and the fuss,
Who cannot play with Spitfire like the boys,
  But bravely clamber on and off the bus.

The young meet lunacy at life's front-door,
  The young have cause to hate the warring Hun:
But that old man has suffered *twice* before,
  And fondly thought that he had saved his son.

And now for him nobody plans or prays;
  That "better world" may come, but he'll be gone.
The young at least can dream of better days,
  With hope and faith and fire to bear them on.

Well done, the old, the uncomplaining breed,
  Who dare not dream except about the past,
But, damn it, man a stirrup-pump at need,
  And keep the flag a-flutter till the last.

August 10, 1941

FIFTY YEARS

(To C. B. Cochran)

For FIFTY YEARS, with pleasures grave and gay,
  You have invited all the world inside
To see the playhouse in its right array—
  A thing of beauty and a place of pride.

And what a fine mixed feast you had to show—
  Ibsen and Coward, Shakespeare, Shaw and all,
Ballet and boxing, Robey and Rodeo,
  Cowboy and Circus!—*and* the Albert Hall!

Reinhardt and Hackenschmidt were one to you;
  Carpentier, Bernhardt, Duse did your will;
Helen of Troy and Jessie of Revue,
  Barrie and Pirandello filled a bill.

Nothing was done because it was "the thing",
  Nothing was done in avarice or haste.
Beauty was Queen, Efficiency was King,
  And over all there ruled the god of Taste.

How much you spent on that Young Lady's shoe
  Was not a worry—if the shoe was right:
How much you made—or lost—you hardly knew
  If only London loved it on "the night".

Alas, how little can the actor keep
  Of all the joy he lavishly distils!
Some faded programmes in the scrap-book sleep—
  A few old photographs—and many bills.

"Who was the man in that delightful play?"
  "Who was the girl who took the leading part?"
Well, never mind. For she has had her day,
  And lives in lodgings with a broken heart.

To men like you we pay no living wage,
  And all their work is swept away like snow.
Yet you have left your footprints on the stage:
  The world is richer for the "Cochran Show".

August 13, 1941

"ROMEO"

THEY MAY NOT fly—we don't know why, for, Heaven
    knows, they can,
And this must be the one thing still monopolised by Man—
So they have done the next best thing (you can't keep good
    girls down),
And women fly a big balloon "somewhere in London
    town".

It's not a "ladies' model". He's as risky as the rest,
As full of tricks and tantrums, not so easily repressed.
You ought to see him yawing like a mad thing in a blow;
You ought to see the winning way they have with
    "Romeo".

And when His Majesty's balloons crowd up to catch the
    Hun,
Like elephants, like sausages, like jewels in the sun,
They say that every sentry in that reassuring row
Makes one respectful curtsy to the only Romeo.

Such wonders swarm about us, we can scarcely feel
    surprise.
But one new wonder very soon may fill the startled skies,
When women fly the big balloons from every shore and
    square,
And many thousand gallant lads are free to take the air.

August 17, 1941

"EACH WAY"

The Atlantic Charter

VE VOS ON a damned good vicket, as der stupid english
say;
If der Fuehrer vin der battle everyting vos quite O.K.
Ve vill haf der eggs and bacon for der Fuehrer vill be just
And der faces of der english ve vos treading in der dust.

If der Fuehrer lose der battle, den der english treat us
good;
Mister Roosevelt, Mister Churchill, dey vos kind and said
dey vould.
Never mind vich way der cat jumps, ve vos safety be both
vay;
Ve vos on der velvet vicket. Heil der Fuehrer! Hip
Hooray.

August 24, 1941

16

ODE ON OIL

OIL!
Beneficent oil,
Mankind's most precious treasure in the soil!
Oil!
Disgusting oil,
Father of blood and sweat and tears and toil!

Oil, you have made this puny race
Masters of Time and Lords of Space,
Have opened vast horizons for the poor,
And brought the city to the cottage door,
Or rather (which is not so good)
The cottage door to Hollywood.
Oil, you have made the mountains and the seas
Mean less than barbed-wire fences mean to bees.
Oil, you have made the Empire one
As even blood could not have done.
Oil, you have scarred the country's face
With hideous roads and buildings base;
Oil, on the other hand,
You fill the fruitful land
With things to eat,
And taught the simple Russians
(After some hot discussions)
How to grow wheat.
Oil, the chief murderer, it's *you* we thank
For aeroplane and submarine and tank.
Oil, you destroyed the Pole,
The Dane, the Dutch, the Greek;
Oil, you support the tyrant sort
And trample on the weak.
I wish you, Oil, at the bottom of the sea—
Which, by the way, is where you used to be.

Odd, is it not?
This cosmic blot,
    Petroleum
(To which is known
One rhyme alone—
    Linoleum),
Prime source of feud and flame,
And all the ills I name,
Is not the drip
From some foul dragon's lip,
    As one would think,
Nor does it flow
From witch-fires far below,
    Where devils drink
    Crude oil and ink—
        No, no!
Quite a long time ago
There played about the surface of the sea
Unnumbered tribes of animalculæ,
    And these, when dead,
(Well, those on whom the fishes did not feed)
    Sank to the deep sea-bed
    And mixed their bones
        With sand and stones
    And waterplant and weed.
        The rivers, too,
        Poured forth into the blue
    Organic silt galore,
        The things that romp
        In stream and swamp,
        Things that are grown
        On each wet stone,
        Starwort and snails,
        And tadpoles' tails,
        Beetles and crabs—

I dare say dabs—
    Algæ,
    And waterflea,
    And one or two more.
Layers of mud then hid the small remains,
Shingle and sand and rocks as big as trains;
Pressure was vast, and, as you've guessed, no doubt,
Carbon and hydrogen were soon about.
The sea-bed heaved—the mud was turned to shale
(Here I'm a little vague about the tale);
Another heave—the shale was thrust ashore,
The mining-engineer began to bore,
And, much to his surprise, good honest soul,
Saw crude petroleum gushing from the hole.

Petrol-e-um! It must have been a shock—
So soft a harvest from so firm a rock!
But that was nothing to the shock he got
When first he boiled a little in the pot.
I used to think that every kind of oil
Had each its own pet section of the soil—
Here petrol bubbled from a petrol-well,
There lubricating oil from heaven fell.
But now I know how much does Heat produce
From this one dirty and adhesive juice.
First the fine petrol creeps into its jar—
And off you go in your capacious car.
Next, paraffin emerges from the vat,
And you may light your little lamps with that.
Thirdly, I *think*, the Diesel oil we note,
With which you shift your motor-barge or boat.
Lastly (though I won't bet on this), we find
The lubricating—or the fuel—kind
With which you fit your tourer for a trip—
Or else you drive a darn great battleship.

And all these boons, remember—'tis my wish—
Proceed from little water-plants and fish.

If I am right—and who will say I'm wrong?—
Maybe this madness will not last for long.
Maybe the small sagacious fish will say,
"There shall be no petroleum to-day."
Maybe once more enlightened Man will hail
The horse, the cart, the rickshaw and the sail;
And Hitler's lads, bereft of tank and plane,
Will have to use the bayonet again.

Methinks I see this writing on the sky:
"Those who by oil have lived by oil shall die."

August 27, 1941

HEIL, HURRY!

Fool at the wheel, rush on, rush on!
Fool on the kerb, rush out!
More than a score will die to-day
A dirty death on the King's highway.
Twenty a day! It's not enough.
Make it thirty—and do your stuff.
Fool at the wheel, rush on, rush on!
Fool on the kerb, rush out!

Step on it, fool, as you pass the school,
　　Step on the old, the slow, the halt!
Dart, silly man, from behind a van,
　　And say it's the lumbering lorry's fault.
Are they so pressing, your small affairs?
You're in a hurry? D'you think God cares?
Will Hitler win, will the Heavens burst
If the man in the sports-car gets there first?
Yes, you are late for your pretty "date"—
But you wouldn't be late if you'd left before.
You think, no doubt, if you scurry about
You'll look important and win the war.
Well, God bless Speed—in a Spitfire, yes!
God bless Speed—in the Scotch express!
But Speed at a cross roads—"saving time"
For a fool in a fret is a first-class crime. . . .
Still, fool at the wheel, rush on, rush on!
Fool on the kerb, why worry,
Nobody cares who's dead and gone,
We die for the great god Hurry.

August 31, 1941

THE DIFFERENCE

HE HAS THE guns, he has the tanks, he has the dirty
    planes;
He has the gold (or so it seems), he has his robber's gains;
But over every citadel the flag of triumph droops,
And General Melancholia's in command of all the troops.

Here (as the papers tell us) Private Optimism's wrong,
And Sergeants Hope and Cheerfulness must never smile
    too long,
And Corporal Complacency may have a nasty fall—
But General Melancholia has no followers at all.

September 7, 1941

THE NINTH POINT

ALL NATIONS are brothers, although they be foes,
And after the war we shall kiss, I suppose.
But the Bulgar should not be expecting too much,
For I can't say I like him as well as the Dutch.

Oh, the Eight Jolly Articles, signed on the sea,
Have promised that all shall be equal and free,
The chaps in the fight and the chaps on the fence—
Which may be most noble, but doesn't make sense.

So the Bulgar had better be wise while he may,
Whatever the Eight Jolly Articles say;
For we shall remember, and do what is right
To the chaps on the fence, and the chaps in the fight.

September 28, 1941

SHALL IT BE GEORGE . . . ?

THEY HAVE NO name, the boys who ride
   The Spitfires round the sky.
We give them all our love and pride
   But call them nothing. Why?

The whole world knows what "Tommies" mean;
   Our "Jack" is everywhere,
With "Joe", His Majesty's Marine—
   But who is that up there?

Shall it be George—or John—or James
   That rides, and rules, the sky?
Well, it must be the best of names
   For it will never die.

October 5, 1941

LUCKY WORD

"To-day's lucky colour is pink.
  To-day's lucky number is one."
But do the astrologers think
  That luck will demolish the Hun?

"To-day's lucky colour is pink."
  But Russia is standing at bay.
And humanity stands on the brink:
  And luck has but little to say.

"To-day's lucky colour is pink."
  But luck never fashioned a plane;
The steamers are shattered and sink,
  And Luck will not build them again. . . .

"To-day's lucky colour is pink—
  To-night's lucky colour is cream."
O, do the astrologers think
  We are quite so insane as we seem?

"To-day's lucky colour is pink."
  But still let the hammers be heard,
For humanity stands on the brink,
  And WORK is the luckiest word.

October 12, 1941

NOT SO CLEVER

I WISH I knew—I wish I knew
  (So many people seem to know)
Exactly what we ought to do
  In order to defeat the foe.

I wish I'd known—I wish I'd known
  Far back in 1921,
As dear old Thompson knew (alone)
  Exactly what we *should* have done.

I wish I'd known, in 1910,
  As Thompson knew—and many more—
What would have been the right way then
  To obviate the present war.

I wish I saw my country's course
  As clear as Robinson and Smith,
And where we ought to land a force
  (And what we ought to land it with).

I wish I knew—I wish I knew,
  Like all the people in the bar,
Why one should strike at Timbuktu,
  And where on earth the Urals are.

And yet I am not much put out;
  For, if we did know such a lot,
We'd be Prime Minister, no doubt—
  And, I confess, I'd rather not.

So I will raise my glass to those
  Who bear the burdens of the day.
They may be frightful fools, God knows,
  But *I* do not and cannot say.

                   October 19, 1941

THE RAILINGS

THEY'RE PULLING all the railings down
  To make the tanks and guns,
And half the eyesores in the town
  Have gone to hurt the Huns.
Old London, as you must allow,
  Looks well without her rails,
And parks are really "public" now
  Which used to look like gaols.

And all the startled people sing,
  "Why must we wait for war?
So very sensible a thing
  Might have been done before."
But when at last we've done the trick,
  And Hitler's down the drain,
Some silly ass is sure to stick
  The railings up again.

October 26, 1941

TO THINK. . . !

To THINK that children used to cry,
 "Oh look, a lovely aeroplane!"
That men were proud that men could fly!
 Will anyone be proud again?

Yes, we'll be proud that British boys
 Were masters, too, of that machine,
And gave the stars a nobler noise,
 And swept the filthy heavens clean.

November 2, 1941

BRING BACK THE BELLS

BRING BACK the bells. The bells are dumb
Until the parachuters come:
And even Huns may be excused
For bombing belfries so abused.
Bring back the bells: for there remains
No music but the aeroplane's
To make us contemplate the sky
And wonder what is what and why.
Let there be steel in Aaron's rod,
And fighters in the ranks of God;
But leave the little church in peace
While we have soldiers and police.

If we can not inform the town
That parachutes are coming down
Without inviting Huns to search
For targets in the parish church,
The old inventive British brain
Had better, surely, think again.
Bring back the bells; and use a drum
To let us know that Hitler's come.
Bring back the bells; for Christmas spells
So many things that sound like bells.

November 7, 1941

FAIR DOES

GREAT STALIN only has to say
   That Hitler cannot win the scrap
And everybody cries, "Hurray!
   That is the spirit! What a chap!"

But when our own bold statesmen bark
   That Hitler must and shall be sunk
Why is it that the same remark
   Is called "Complacency" or "Bunk"?

November 9, 1941

THE QUEEN IN PARLIAMENT

I CANNOT say why—
But the Queen made me cry.

She sat by the King,
She said not a thing:
She said not a word,
But every heart stirred.
His job was not fun,
But the job was well done.
He did it alone—
But *she* sat by the throne.
Then he gave her his arm—
Grace, dignity, charm,
And a spirit so rare
There was joy in the air.
She curtsied, she smiled,
Like a queen—like a child.
She said not a word,
But every heart stirred;
And when they withdrew
Every heart went out too.
The King, with his men,
Opened Parliament then:
But the Queen opened more—
British women at war.

I think I know why
The Queen made me cry.

November 16, 1941

THE BATTLE OF BOREDOM

He said, "I blustered, but they did not quake."
  He said, "I blasted, but they did not creep.
The more I do, the more they are awake;
  So I will send the silly fools to sleep.

"They seem to think that fighting fires is fun!
  So they shall watch for nothing, dusk to dawn.
I cannot get the British race to run:
  But I can beat the British if they yawn."

So let the dullest heart contrive to leap,
  And every dustman wear a shining sword.
While Hitler triumphs not one soul can sleep:
  While Hitler lives no Briton can be bored.

November 23, 1941

TO W. S. C.

(The Prime Minister is sixty-seven to-day)

MANY HAPPY RETURNS of the day
 To the father of purpose and plan,
To the one who was first in the fray,
 Never doubted, or rested, or ran,
To the Voice of old Britain at bay,
 To the Voice of young men in the van,
To the Voice of new worlds on the way—
 To "We must—and we will—and we can!"
May he live to hear History say,
 "This was their finest man".

November 30, 1941

THE COSMIC MESS

AT LAST the bogies of our youth
Become a large, unlovely truth.
The Swiss and (for the moment) Spain
May still, officially, be sane;
But there is not one sea or shore
Can say, "We are not in *this* war".
And Lloyd's for all their loving care
Will not insure you anywhere.
Like some dark legend from the past
The Yellow Peril lives at last;
And all the heavens look like hells
Conceived by Tennyson—or Wells.
The startled gods may well decide
To have the planet certified;
Or send a comet down to fry
The only scandal in the sky.
Yet we have reason to believe,
The gods have something up their sleeve.
The Russians do not seem to know
That they were finished months ago.
Old China gaily goes ahead,
Quite unaware that she is dead;
And courage still, and kindliness
Illuminate the cosmic mess
(While, by the way, the total score
Is now one continent to *four*!).
The tricksy Jap may think he's won
By getting off before the gun—

And the unsportsmanlike device
Of eating nothing much but rice.
But, though the odds be none too bright,
I put my money on The Right.

December 14, 1941

TO EIRE

MAJESTIC EIRE, all alone
You sit your sad, superior throne,
And note—with some disdain, no doubt—
The foolish warring world about.
Of bad old England no one could
Say anything that sounded good;
And naturally you ignore
Her crude Imperialistic war.
But can you still sit still and grin
When the United States join in,
Dear peaceful virtuous Uncle Sam
Who used to kiss you in your pram,
And always understood the kid
Much better than her mother did?
Well, yes, you can. And may you be
Always so fortunate and free!
Majestic enviable land,
Good luck to you! It must be grand.

December 21, 1941

LOVE YOUR HUNS

I'M A LITTLE bit tired of the chaps who proclaim
    That all are to blame for the war,
And if only we all would acknowledge our shame
    There wouldn't be war any more.

I may be old-fashioned, I may be absurd,
    I may be un-Christian, perhaps;
But I shyly suggest that the parties who erred
    Were the Wops, and the Huns, and the Japs.

I'm told that the Wop and the Jap and the Hun
    Are fellow-men, misunderstood;
And so I should love them, whatever they've done.
    Well, I try. But it isn't much good.

I'm told that the Germans are mammals like me,
    Just a few simple sweet fellow souls;
But I cannot help thinking—I hope you agree—
    It was Germans who murdered the Poles.

And any poor fish who can't make up his mind
    Who began it—the Hun or the Czech;
Well, he may be exceedingly gentle and kind
    But he gives me a pain in the neck.

I know that I must be forgiving and just,
    But the Japs are beginning to pall,
My love for the Wop is a bit of a flop
    And I cannot love Hitler at all.

December 28, 1941

WELL DONE, THE DUTCH!

WELL DONE, the Dutch! Though Hitler's hand
Fell heavy on the motherland
They did not whisper, as it fell,
"Pray take our colonies as well".
They said: "Do not assume too much.
We're sailors still." Well done, the Dutch!

Well done, the Dutch! When larger chaps
Were talking big, but taking naps,
They put to sea and handed slaps
To the insufferable Japs.
We did not like the Van Tromp touch—
We like it now. Well done, the Dutch!

January 4, 1942

CHILD'S GUIDE TO MODERN
WARFARE

Q.: "What happens, Daddy, in an open town?"
A.: "The hands go up, my boy—the bombs come down."

January 4, 1942

THE CHANGING TUNE*

The tune is changed. In '41
His war, he promised, must be won.
To-day he *prays* that God will do
His dirty work in '42.
Next New Year may the Message be
"God spare my neck in '43".
And (if there must be any more)
"Forgive me, God," in '44.

January 4, 1942

* Hitler's New Year oration.

THE GIRLS OF THE NEW BRIGADE

(*Air*—"Boys of the Old Brigade")

WHERE ARE the Girls of the New Brigade?
 Wherever the old flag flies.
Members of many a strange new trade
 They're there till the Bad Man dies.
They'll fall in, all, for the Last Parade,
 And whether they're blue or brown,
The gay grim Girls of the New Brigade
 Will have little Hitler down.

Merrily we go about the business,
Singing in the sun—or shade,
Working away,
Gallant and gay,
Are the Girls of the New Brigade.

Where are the Girls of the New Brigade?
  Where there's a job to do.
Give them a saucepan—a shell—a spade—
  And they will see you through.
They'll shop till they drop, if it stops That Man,
  And type till the world is free;
They'll stand in queues till they've no more shoes,
  And laugh when there's no more tea:

> *Merrily we go about the business,*
>   *Singing in the sun—or shade,*
>   *Quick to the call,*
>   *Lipstick and all,*
>   *Are the Girls of the New Brigade.*

Where are the Girls of the New Brigade?
  Where there's a job to be done.
Where's the machine to be manned—or made;
  Something to hit the Hun?
We'll drive a tank, or control a bank,
  A bus—a balloon—a man!
We mean to see that the world is free.
  We must—and we will—and we can.

> *Merrily we go about the business,*
>   *Singing in the sun—or shade,*
>   *Friendly and frank,*
>   *Tough as a tank,*
>   *Are the Girls of the New Brigade.*

January 16, 1942

"MORAL"

"This war
Is a bore."
Yes, we don't want no more.
But we'll win this old war, as we won it before;
And until little Hitler is flat on the floor
Let no man ignore
That we're all for
The war.

"This war
Is a bore."
There are hearts sick and sore.
Tom's earning a tanner, but Ted's earning more.
They don't seem to have what we want at the store.
The Jap's at the door of that darn Singapore,
And sometimes we wonder what Singapore's *for*.
But united we roar
That we're all for
The war.

"This war,
Is a bore."
There must be no encore.
Cheer up. There are signs that we're ceasing to snore.
There are not many "avenues" left to "explore".
The Yankees awake, like the Yankees of yore:
The Russians, though red, are more white than before;
The Navy's on top from the Nile to the Nore;
We've made a fair mess of the Afrika Korps.
The motto for moaners is "Excelsior!
Every man to the charge, every girl to the chore!"

And if Goebbels and Goering should jaw any more
  In chorus we'll roar,
    "We're all for
     The war!"

January 18, 1942

FREEZE ON. . . !

I HAVE the most insanitary cold;
I feel rheumatic, bronchial, and old.
I do not find this kind of weather fun—
But how much worse it must be for the Hun!

I do not like the slush through which we tramp;
I do not like my blankets *quite* so damp;
I do not like the way my nose will run—
But how much worse it must be for the Hun!

The wild wind whistles through my tender hide,
And comes out, whistling still, the other side.
But I almost delight to have this done—
For how much worse it must be for the Hun!

Freeze on, freeze on, thou bitter, bitter sky!
Freeze on, freeze on, if need be till July!
Freeze on, freeze on, until the world is free,
And never mind if it distresses me.
No one is shooting at us with a gun—
Oh, how much worse it must be for the Hun!

PS. No, never mind. Freeze—thaw—do what you will;
For, freeze or not, the Hun will get a chill.
Though it were sweltering from Pole to Pole,
There'd still be icicles in Hitler's soul.

January 25, 1942

O.S.T.

I SING with warm, unworthy lips
The praises of Sir Stafford Cripps.
Well done—and welcome—man of mark,
Who laboured nobly in the dark,
And now that Russia shows a ray,
Deserve the laurels of the day!
For though, no doubt, it's Hitler whom
We'll have to thank for Hitler's doom,
You must have made the Russians see
How honest Englishmen can be.
Some Russians must have learned from you
That Britons can be Modern, too;
And this is odd, because you wore
(Like Halifax and Samuel Hoare)
An ornament that all decry—
I mean, of course, the Old School Tie.

How could a knight with such a flag
Expect such booty in the bag?
A school five hundred years of age!
Was this the stuff for such a stage—
One of those fossilising spots
From which come only blimps or blots?
Did you discuss with Premier Joe
Those cricket matches long ago?
Does the great Stalin know or dream
You captained once a football team?
Well, well, in spite of that sad past
You warmed the Russian heart at last,
And possibly that ancient Hall
Was not so dusty, after all.

You wear the Tie that Wavell wore
And Portal—and a good few more.
(While you, at least, will not omit
The name of our old playmate, Pritt.)

I never quite can understand
Why love and loyalty are grand
If it's trade unions and their rules
But not if it is people's schools.
Trade union buttons everywhere
The same proud sentiments declare,
And little difference I can see
In O.S.T. and T.U.B.
In fact, as history will tell,
They wear together pretty well.
At all events, with friendly lips,
Let us salute Sir Stafford Cripps:
For when some other job's begun
We know it will be darn well done;
And I am very proud that I
May also wear his old school tie.

PS.   And maybe Hoare and Halifax
Do not deserve such dirty cracks.

February 1, 1942

BUS-DRIVER

Bus-driver, bus-driver, we wait by the lamp;
We stare up the street and we swear and we stamp.
Bus-driver, bus-driver, we look for your light
And bless, as it breaks, the one star in the night.

Bus-driver, bus-driver, how bravely you steam
Like a very great ship in a very small stream—
Every refuge a reef, every shadow a snare—
Missing idiots by inches, old men by a hair!

Bus-driver, we board you, a shivering queue;
We're safe and snug now—and forget about you.
But on through the darkness you rumble and sway,
With a suicide waiting each yard of the way—
All alone on the bridge, with no man to admire,
As you save a few lives by the skin of a tyre—
Missing idiots by inches, old men by a hair—
Every refuge a reef, every shadow a snare!
Bus-driver, I know you won't think me a snob
If I whisper, "Bus-driver, I don't want your job."

February 8, 1942

SOAP

You will forgive me, Phyllis, I am sure:
My hands are filthy, but my heart is pure.
I know how often I have worn this shirt;
But, please recall, it's patriotic dirt.
Remember, statesmen, if our speech seems raw,
Too much soft soap is now against the law.
I dare say Hitler washes pretty well,
But in his mind is all the muck of Hell.
He does not smoke or drink, or swallow meat,
But lives on death, disloyalty, deceit;
And, when at last we whisk him from the scene,
Our hands will reek—our conscience will be clean.

"ADMIRALS ALL"

Napoleon's soldiers—remarked the old wag—
Have a Field-Marshal's baton in every bag:
But our Man-in-the-street, it is easy to tell,
Has an Admiral's flag in his pocket as well.

Oh, it's cheering to hear, in the bus and the bar,
What a lot of Field-Marshals and Admirals we are!
But perhaps, till we're called to take charge of the show,
We had better get on with some job that we know.

February 22, 1942

43

TOADS IN THE HOLE

We're in a hole, a deep dark hole. It's not much use to
    shout;
Though anyone's in order who explains how we get
    out.
We're sure to have some sickening slips before we've done
    the climb,
But will it help to halt and hold an inquest every time?
(I don't suppose that Hitler would appoint a High Court
    Judge
To inquire into the reasons why the Russians will not
    budge.)
Nor do we need the little toads, the small anæmic souls
Who sigh that we are sinners and deserve to be in holes;
For though, no doubt, like others, we are capable of sin
The essence of the story is that someone pushed us in;
And though the hole grows deeper till it's half-way down
    to Hell
We'll catch that fellow one fine day and throw him down
    a well.
Meanwhile, I think I see a rope descending from the sky:
And if I'm very wrong, brave boys, by gad, we'll have to
    fly!
I also see a mighty man who holds the other end:
And anyone who knocks him on the head is not my friend.

February 22, 1942

ST. DAVID'S DAY

PERHAPS, AS clever people like to cry,
"This nationality" is all my eye;
Perhaps there should be only one great race;
Perhaps all local saints are out of place,
And David, Patrick, George should leave the map
To one big International Good Chap.
No one but God could tell us why He grows
The daffodil so different from the rose:
They may be right who prophesy our doom
Unless we've One Co-ordinated Bloom.
But if we must so doubtfully discuss
The various elements that flavour us,
Well, I, for one, most happily proclaim
Our pepper, mustard, salt are NOT the same;
And here is one who reverently hails
The flags, the flowers—and the fruits—of Wales.

March 1, 1942

TO J. L. GARVIN

THE LITTLE FELLOWS laughed that you were long;
The feeble fellows never like the strong;
The crooked creatures do not love the straight—
But all, I think, agreed that you were great.

You did not always rollick or rejoice,
But all the time you spoke with England's voice.
Though rude men talked about "The Cliveden Set",
Nobody asked, "Which way does Garvin bet?"

Newspapers get new masters in a night;
But it takes more to teach a man to write.
So we shall miss the thunder and the flame,
And Sunday mornings will not be the same.

March 11, 1942

COLONEL BLIMP

An Epitaph

HERE LIES poor Blimp, the target of the town—
Still more alive than some who ran him down.
I never met the man. Nor do I know
Why all the clever lads disliked him so.
To be a Colonel, after all, is not
Conclusive evidence that one's a blot:
In fact, I find, in Service or in shop,
It's not for nothing that men reach the top.

"Old-fashioned warrior," cry Smith and Jones,
Whose only form of fight is throwing stones.
Far back, he wanted England to be strong;
But even then the bright boys thought him wrong.
"Warmonger" was the name they gave him then,
Signing "Peace Ballots" with a golden pen.
Let them confess, the lazy and the limp,
That no Peace Ballot bore the name of Blimp.
Indeed, the day the tiger springs my way
I'd just as soon that Blimp was there as they.

March 8, 1942

HONG-KONG

GOD USED to strike those yellow men
  More cruelly than mortals can:
To think that we were sorry then
  And sent our pennies to Japan!

To-day we must not hate the foe
  Nor promise punishment for sins.
"Vengeance is mine," says God, we know:
  And we must wait till that begins.

But I, at least, could not refrain
  From just one crude, unworthy crow
If thunder shook those shores again
  And made a tomb of Tokyo.

March 15, 1942

WARSHIPS WEEK

In every creek and river, wherever ships could ride,
King Alfred's men built ships for him and sent them
    down the tide;
And many a modest stream, boys, and many a humble
    street
Were proud they'd sent a *Monarch* or a *Glory* to the Fleet.
To-day the little places lay famous keels no more:
No battleship is building from Chiswick to the Nore.
But we can still contrive, boys, that every tiny town
Shall help to make an *Exeter*, a *Cossack*, or *Renown*.
It may be "ballyhoo", boys, as clever people say:
The Navy won't go short, maybe, if you refuse to pay.
But we can all be partners in this tremendous thing;
And I *like* to think I'm lending a *Cossack* to the King.

March 22, 1942

SPRING SONG

Or, The Poet in Difficulties

I MUST NOT say, "The day is fine and hot."
That is complacency: so I will not.

I must not say, "The day is cold and wet."
That is despondency—more deadly yet.

I must not say, "The sky is grey and solemn."
That is defeatist—and perhaps Fifth Column.

And, if from every comment I refrain,
That's dangerous apathy, and wrong again.

I must not say, "There may be storms ahead."
That is a rumour, and must not be spread.

And then, I must not give our enemies
The smallest hint of what the weather *is*.

Nor should I say what flowers (if any) grow,
For any trifle may assist the foe.

So, with all proper reticence, I sing
That, by the date, I *think* it must be Spring.

WISE GUYS

OF ALL THE puzzles put to man,
  Of all the courses queer to plot,
Of all the futures hard to plan—
  I take it, India beats the lot.

But, though it baffles me and you,
  Spectators seem to see right through it:
For all the world knows what to do
  Except the ones who have to do it.

And I, for one, delight to know
  That farmers in the Middle West,
Or Montreal, or Mexico,
  Could say exactly what was best.

But does the wise world never ask,
  When it requires new Constitutions,
How Hitler would attack the task
  Or what would be the Jap solutions?

Well, well, till folly's had its fill,
  We'll keep the flag of patience flying:
The world will keep on talking still,
  While poor old Britain keeps on trying.

April 5, 1942

STORKS MUST LIVE

"Please, Mr. Chancellor, a present for the stork?
You can't build Britons, not without a knife and fork.
Please, Mr. Chancellor, it's really time you did.
Well, anyone would think it was a crime to have a
kid.
Yet they're yapping and they're yelling that the race is
running out.
In a hundred years, they say, there won't be nobody
about.

"Well, I'm a good mother, and I'd *like* to have another;
But while he's on the way, sir, who is going to mind his
brother?
For Matilda's in the Waafs, and Maria's in the Wrens,
And them that can do women's work is busy doing
men's.
And then there's little Mabel, well, she's very fond of
Harry,
But is that right, Chancellor, you'll *tax* them if they
marry?

"It's a job to keep alive, sir, if you're only one or two.
There's the rent, there's the rations, there's the shopping
and the queue.
The stork's a British bird, sir, and keen to do his best;
But he needs a little nourishment, he needs a little nest.
He don't ask for oysters, he don't insist on pork:
But *please*, Mr. Chancellor, a present for the stork?"

April 12, 1942

THE 45's

Too old at 45, sir? This is hard—
A volunteer so soon from battle barred!
At 20, when you did not know a thing,
You were thought fit to soldier for the King.
At 24, when you had won a war
You knew as much as Wellington—and more.
In '39, when Freedom stood at bay,
Few regiments, I think, said, "Go away!"
But now, when, Lord knows why, brooms must be new,
So sorry, but we have no use for you.
You must go back to businesses and banks,
But some of us, at least, are thinking, "Thanks";
And when those Huns do take the London Train
Maybe we'll see you with a gun again.

April 19, 1942

HITLER'S BIRTHDAY

Or, Many Jolly Lavals!

Unlike Napoleon, you are 53;
And Berlin beams—or doesn't it—with glee.
The whole world makes a suitable salute,
With special gestures from the Russian boot.
But there's not anyone who calls you pal
Except perhaps a certain Pierre Laval;
And fate, most fitly, celebrates your birth
By giving you the nastiest man on earth.

April 19, 1942

"WAIT FOR IT"

(as the Sergeant says)

"WAIT FOR IT, wait for it", fidgety Phil!
Before you can march you must learn to stand still.
"Wait for it", lad. Better walk before run;
And before you can kill you must handle a gun.
"Wait for it", soldiers. You've waited too long?
But waiting's not weak—it's the test of the strong.

"Wait for it", Russia. You know what we've done;
But there's very much more we shall do to the Hun.
"Wait for it", Frenchmen, and Dutchmen, and Danes!
We are making great hammers to shatter your chains.

"Wait for it", Hitler—the weather may mend,
But from ocean to ocean you haven't a friend;
And wherever you thrust your inflammable snout
You have lit a volcano you'll never put out.
"Wait for it", sentry on every shore;
For any fine morning may find you no more.

"Wait for it", world. The old lion was late;
But the lion's as sure, and as savage, as Fate.
You may twist his old tail—you may think he is dumb;
But "wait for it", Fritz—he will come, he will come.

April 26, 1942

"YOU WILL BE SORRY"

STOP SQUEALING "Rostock". Think of Rotterdam,
   And see if you have grown a sense of shame.
Then think of Warsaw—Coventry—East Ham.
   You will be sorry you began this game.
Do you remember Rotterdam, you brute?
   You thought you'd made a monster none could tame.
You thought you'd got the globe beneath your boot.
   Well, you'll be sorry you began this game.
Though all the stars in Baedeker go down,
   And half the things we love go up in flame,
You'll wonder why you ever touched a town—
   You will be sorry you began this game.

May 3, 1942

THE BROWN FLAG

WELL DONE, the bold guerrillas, who bear no badge or
    flag
But may "be just as good" at putting dragons in the bag!
"Then why not all guerrillas—independent all the time—
An Independent Party—with an Independent Prime?"
Well, child, the notion's charming; but the best guerrillas
    know
You need some regiments as well to finish off the foe.
And though the boys who bound along alone have lots
    of pep
There *is* a use for one or two who've learned to march in
    step.

May 3, 1942

ODE ON THE NAMES OF STARS

LET US RENAME the stars. The ancient names
Are not sufficient for the cosmic flames.
The Arab steered his course across the sand
Keeping *Achernar* on his starboard hand.
 He held his camel's head
 On *Skat* or *Tarazed*.
He fed his camel and lay down to rest
When *Alpheratz* was bearing North by West.
 When *Nath* no more was seen
 He knew the corn was green:
 When *Nath* was seen again
 He cut the golden grain.
  He knew *Mizar*,
 He knew *Alshain*,
 And *Sadalsund*, the lucky star,
  That brought soft rain.
He knew *Mirzam* and *Alnilam*,
  The pearly string,
 He knew *Menkalinan*,
 Aldebaran,
 And *Sheratan*,
  The star of Spring.
But what is *Alchiba* to you and me,
Diphda the Frog, or *Deneb Algedi*?
I cannot summon interest in *Skat*,
In *Phact*, or *Saiph*, or *Chaph*, or *Sulaphat*.
In vain *Alphacca* twinkles up and down,
"The brightest pearl in Ariadne's crown".
I do not know her. I should not complain
If *Alchiba* was never seen again.

  And then, up there
There are too many animals, I swear.

Why all these Goats, Sheep, Scorpions, and Dogs,
These Beaks of Hens, and Fish's Mouths, and Frogs?
    Are these fit signs for such a sight,
    The million torches of the night,
      To which poor men
      Turn now and then
    For Light?
We must have nobler-sounding stars
    To man the heavenly deck.
These are more fit for cocktail-bars—
    Indeed, there *is* a star called *Horse's Neck*.

We might keep *Sirius*, *Capella* too,
Virgo and *Vega*, beacon brave and blue,
Castor and *Pollux*—these are names we know;
But *Betelgeuse* and *Benetnasch* must go.
And even then, maybe, there's too much Rome:
Let us have stars that make us feel at home!
    Instead of *Draco, Drake*—
    A Seaman for a Snake.
    Nay, let the seamen take
      Orion's square,
For that's a signal sailors know most well,
And every star in it a tale should tell—
Beatty for *Betelgeuse*—*Harwood* for *Rigel*—
Nelson for *Saiph*—and as for *Alnilam*,
Well, why not *Vian, Hawke* or *Cunningham*?
There's room for eight or nine good admirals there.
    The Army too should have its heavenly pitch.
      I know not which,
      But they might go
      To *Scorpio*,
Where red *Antares*, giant of the stars,
    Defies red *Mars*.

Aye, there must be more Britain in the sky.
    I can't think why
The Senior Constellation,
    Absurdly called *The Bear*,
Circling without cessation
    In British air,
Should not be *ours*—the Seven Stars that keep
Their nightly watch while Britons sleep,
Nor ever sneak away into the south,
Like the *Crow's Whiskers* or the *Fish's Mouth*!
Great Bear? Great *Bear*? I here and now proclaim—
Great Britain is the constellation's name:
And all the Seven shall carry round the Pole
The blazing name of some great English soul:
Shakespeare, Elizabeth, Milton, whom you will—
Churchill, maybe, for we have great men still.
    Mind you, I'd not expel
        All other nations.
    America shall swell
        The League of Constellations—
We'll give her *Aquila*, with grand *Altair*.
    Russia shall fly
    Her Sickle in the sky—
Look, does not *Leo* hang a sickle there?
        She shall have, too,
        Fair *Ursa Minor*, who
Is much more like a Hammer than a Bear.
    Draco for China—thus these four shall lie
    In noble line across the Northern sky.
    Lyra, with lovely *Vega*, to France I give,
    Aye, you shall see
    The names of all the free
Flame in the firmament of Peace—
    Though I know not
    What star we've got

That's bright enough for Greece.
    Even the Wops,
    When all this nonsense stops,
    May flicker, I dare say,
    In some dim corner of the Milky Way.
        But not one Hun, and not one Jap
        (Much as I love a hostile chap)—
    Not for a long, long day!

        And above all shall shine
        New stars, a splendid line,
            For some whose claim
            None will deny
            To have their name
            Always on high—
            The boys who fly,
            And fight, and die,
        To keep the heavens clean,
        Bader and *Kain*,
            Cliff, *Malan*, *Finucane*,
    With all their golden brothers
        Who will be or have been.

So shall our children, heavenward gazing,
    See more than we have seen,
See more than beacons coldly blazing
    With names that nothing mean—
The soul of man forever striving
    To break the bars—
The noblest work of God's contriving.
    Christen the stars!
                                    May 6, 1942

59

WE WERE THE FIRST . . .

Ah, yes, we are lazy, and foolish, and fat;
  And nothing we do is just what it should be:
And Russia does this, and America that—
  But we were the first to fight for the free.

For twenty-five years we've done everything wrong,
  And no wonder the clever ones giggle with glee;
For we tried to be kind, and we failed to be strong—
  Yet we were the first to fight for the free.

So let the bright fellows make hay with our fame!
  This is the truth the simple can see;
This is the claim that will cling to our name;
This is the boast that no beating can shame;
This is the picture our children will frame—
We did not wait till the enemy came:
  We were the first to fight for the free.

May 10, 1942.

"DRAW IT MILD"

"Justice for Germany", the good men plead.
No, No, that would be barbarous indeed!
Justice to Prussia? Justice to the Hun?
We could not be so harsh to anyone.

May 10, 1942

HOME GUARD BIRTHDAY

Home Guard, with all salutes we light
Two candles on your cake to-night.
We wish, we hope we use you, well,
For what a tale will history tell!

You watch by dark, you work by day;
You serve with pride, but not with pay;
The greatest army known to fame
That did not care when Friday came.

On Sunday, when the soldiers rest,
You get a gun and give your best.
One day alone is your big day—
The day the Prussians come your way.
But we may still take leave to light
Two candles on your cake to-night.

May 17, 1942

THE CAPTIVE BALLOON

Or, Duce far Niente

AND SO, Top Wop, you're giving tongue again!
"Corsica—Tunis—Nice—" the old refrain.

Across the fence how cockily you crow,
Knowing your neighbour has no stones to throw.

But what a bankrupt buccaneer you look—
The man who hitched his wagon to a crook!

You can cock snooks at Pétain and Laval:
But will you lift a finger to your pal?

Before you snatch at someone else's throne,
Why not remove the bailiffs from your own?

Before you start in management at Nice
Why not try managing your own police?

Are you so sure it's France you should attack?
Why not begin by getting Italy back?

May 24, 1942

HEYDRICH

I AM so sorry Heydrich has been shot.
I liked the little reptile quite a lot.
No, "like" is not the word. I *loved* the swine—
As I must love all enemies of mine.
I do not think the Russians or the Dutch
Love Himmler and his fellow monsters much.
But we are British, nobler than the rest,
And we must love this unexampled pest.
We are the British, and, the worse they do,
The more we love these weasels—well, don't you?
We can be kind, and just, and chivalrous
About the things they have not done to us.
It's true they massacre the Czech, the Pole:
They break his bones, and (if they can) his soul.
It's true the crimes that stand against their name
Might sting old Satan to a sense of shame.
It's true the victims take another view;
But we love thugs and torturers. Don't you?
Though it's our job to blow them all to Hell,
We must be working for their good as well;
We hunt our foxes for the foxes' good.
(No wonder Britons are misunderstood!)
And so, dear Czechs, Herr Heydrich must not die
For he may be a good boy by and by.
Don't shoot beloved Himmler through the head.
Give him a chance, old chap.   Shoot low instead.

May 31, 1942

SOMETHING RIGHT . . .

"THERE MUST be something wrong", the philosophers say,
  "Or why is man forever in the mud?
Only the beast and bully can get their way.
  And even the infants have a taste for blood.
All, all our art and aim is doing ill,
  And there are tears from Hackney to Hong-Kong.
Now we have learned to chuckle while we kill!
  There must be something wrong."

"There must be something wrong," the patriots cry,
  "For there are rogues and ruffians in the news,
And there are blunders nobody can deny,
  And there are scandals nobody could excuse.
This man is shirking, while the next one sweats,
  And Bedlam is the place where we belong—
Look what that boy of Mrs. Thomson's gets!
  There must be something wrong."

Yet, when I think of England standing at bay,
  Holding her tiny torch in a world gone black,
Facing the devil in mass, a channel away,
  And thinking of nothing still but hitting him back;
And when I think of the friend of the free to-day
  Arming the giant and leading the lost to light,
I look at the stars and say, as the simple say,
  "*There must be something right.*"

June 7, 1942

TOT-AL WAR

(A new currency has been given to the ominous phrase
heard in 1917 and 1918: *"Wir siegen uns tot"*—"We are
    killing ourselves by our victories."—*The Times*.)

THE HEN-ROOSTS of Europe are held by the Hun,
And, if trespassing counts as a win, he has won:
But the chickens are choking the old fox's throat
And his litter, they jitter: *"Wir siegen uns tot."*

The New Order organ may peal through the town,
But one note, a deep one, is always stuck down:
"We've won—but we're done," says that obstinate note,
"From conquer to canker—*Wir siegen uns tot.*"

June 14, 1942

THE RED FAG

GAY GIRL, brave girl, we like the way you walk,
So proud a flower on so slight a stalk;
We love the way you wear your uniform,
Like a small ship rigged ready for the storm;
We love the way you march into the war,
As if you'd been in several wars before.
But we *don't* like the way you do your lips,
So far from comely—and so far from Cripps!
You move about the world like some pink snail,
Leaving a small but very sticky trail.
The cigarette you suck, the glass you drain,
The cake you nibble, have the same foul stain:
And the bold beau who takes you out to dine
Should take as well a little turpentine.
The savage does not paint his face, we know,
To please his friends, but petrify the foe:
If that's the notion in your handsome head
Then all the Germans are as good as dead.
But you're too fresh to need another face,
And you're so fine that faking's a disgrace.
You are too pretty to rely on paint,
You are so wise that you should learn restraint.
Gay girl, brave girl, I know what you will say,
That men, poor idiots, like you best that way.
No, no, on this all mortal men agree—
Though few, I fancy, are as brave as me.

June 21, 1942

SECOND INNINGS*

ONE DAY we bowled out Rommel for a blob,
But no one said, "Let's throw him to the mob."
No one, I think, debated loud and long
The many reasons why the man was wrong.

No clever fellow sent him from the City
A vote of censure on the whole Committee.
Nobody yelled, "His competence is partial."
They made the blasted fellow a Field-Marshal.

Nobody said, "This batsman should be shot."
He went in first again—and made a lot.
Nor will we throw our captain down the drain.
The bowling's good. But we shall bat again.

June 28, 1942

* Before the Vote of Censure—and Alamein.

COME ON!

THEY SAY that we are listless in the fight,
   They say the bugles do not move us now;
They say St. George cares less about the Right;
   They say the lion has become a cow.

It is not true. We know it is not true.
   We know that we are set to do or die.
But let them sound the bugle calls anew—
   Come on, and let us show the world they lie.

July 5, 1942

FREE SPEECH

("So far as I am concerned, if I had to choose between Hitler and the Prime Minister, I should not know exactly on which the choice had to fall."—An Honourable Member in the Debate on the Vote of Censure.)

For this did God contrive the human brain,
   For this our sailors face the awful sea,
For this boys perish on the Libyan plain,
   That thought be sacred and that speech be free.
This is the right your fathers won for you—
But you who use it have some duties too.

July 5, 1942

"AFTER THE WAR"

"I DON'T SEE," said William, "just how we shall win:
In fact I'd be glad if I saw us begin.
But they tell me that don't worry no one no more,
For the one thing that matters is 'after the war'.
Well, I wouldn't have guessed, but from all that I've
   heard
This old war is the best thing as ever occurred.
When you think how much better we're going to be—
Them Utopias is nothing as far as I see.
And if you say 'William, how can that be so?'
Well, there, I'm that ignorant I wouldn't know.

> *Oh, won't it be wonderful after the war?—*
> *There won't be no war, and there won't be no pore.*
> *We won't have to work if we find it a bore,*
> *We'll all get a pension about 24,*
> *And there's only one problem I'd like to explore—*
>   *Why didn't we have the old wa-er before?*

"It ain't against Hitler we're fighting, they say,
But the Economic System what led him astray.
It ain't the nice Germans what murders the Poles,
But them old Vested Interests as poisons their souls.
Poor Hitler of rubber and oil was bereft,
So we'll give him what rubber and oil we've got left;
And this here arrangement will end, as you'll see,
In a much better world both for you and for me.
But if you say 'William, how can that be so?'
Well, there, I'm that ignorant I wouldn't know.

> *But won't it be wonderful after the war?—*
> *We'll all have a carriage-and-four at the door.*
> *There won't be no sick, and there won't be no sore,*
> *The beer will be better, and quicker, and more;*

There's only one question shakes me to the core—
Why didn't we have the old wa-er before?

"If there's one thing we're sick of, it's the State, there's
   no doubt—
All them cards, and inspectors, and messing about;
If there's one sort of snake we'd all send to the Zoo
It's them uncivil servants and burrowcrats too.
But in this new Heaven and Earth what's ahead
There'll be nothing but nationalising, it's said,
Which means the ole world will be run in Whitehall,
And before we know what we'll be burrowcrats all.
But if you say 'William, how can that be so?'
Well, there, I'm that ignorant I wouldn't know.

   "Oh, won't it be wonderful after the war?
   There won't be no rich, and there won't be no pore.
   We'll work for the State, and we'll knock off at four,
   And we won't work at all if we find it a bore.
   There won't be no sick, and there won't be no sore;
   The beer will be better, and quicker, and more;
   And there's only one avenue I'd like to explore—
   Why didn't we have the old wa-er before?"

                                        July 8, 1942

The refrain goes rather movingly to "The Mountains o' Mourne".

70

LITTLE SHOP

Little merchant, little dealer, little sweet-and-paper
    shop,
They say you've got to go—but I should like to see you
    stop.
You knew just what I wanted, and I wanted what you'd
    got;
You did your best to have it, and were sorry if you'd not.
Besides, you were a neighbour; your address was not the
    Ritz;
You were born behind the shop—and nearly died there
    in the blitz.

There's not one of us gets married, joins the Forces,
    fights the foe,
That didn't toddle in to you for ice-cream cornets long
    ago.
But we liked to think our pennies went to somebody we
    knew;
We like to feel we're something more than customers to
    you.

But I don't remember meeting many chain-stores in the
    pub,
And there's not a joint-stock company will join the
    skittles club.
You've got no proper economic function, so I hear;
But a Company's no company—and seldom buys a beer.
Little merchant, little dealer, little sweet-and-paper
    shop—
Damn the old "economics"! I should like to see you stop.

July 12, 1942

BLOCKWARTS

(A *Blockwart*—German for Block Warden—is the official
responsible to the Nazi Party for the block of houses or
flats in which he lives.)

IN EVERY BLOCK, in every street,
   Where Uncle Himmler has his way
Some *Blockwart* walks on rubber feet
   To watch, to listen, to betray.

Stout hearts, in fear, their friends forsake
   And shepherds fear to call their sheep,
And weary people keep awake
   For fear they whisper in their sleep.

So when our jelly-bellies bleat,
   "How are we better than the Hun?"
Say, "There's no *Blockwart* in this street—
   And when there is, we'll get a gun!"

"And we will never let them be,
   And we will never rest, we swear,
Till we can shout from sea to sea—
   There are no *Blockwarts* anywhere!"

July 14, 1942

WELCOME, DOUGHBOY!

WELCOME, DOUGHBOY! Once again
   Freedom's peril brings you over;
California—Kansas—Maine
   Face the same old foe at Dover.

All the past, and all the pleas,
   All the braying, all the blame,
Could not keep you from the seas—
   Freedom beckoned, and you came.

China's weary, Russia's worn,
   You are young, and we are small;
But the bully is not born
   That can stand against us all.

Yet we are not through the wood;
   Therefore, Doughboy, thanks a lot!
You have given us all you could:
   We must give you all we've got.

Pumpkin pie? Iced water? Nay.
   But a heart that's tough and true,
And, whatever people say,
   Slightly democratic too.

Welcome, Doughboy! Hand in hand
   We will tour Berlin and Rome:
And till then this ancient land
   Hopes that you may feel at home.

July 19, 1942

SECOND FRONT

(*To a Fierce Young Critic*)

YOUR SPIRIT'S great, young man—your mind is meagre.
  Try to accept the charitable view
That Mr. Churchill may be just as eager
  To take the war to Germany as you.

July 19, 1942

FINUCANE

AT 21 YOU touched the top:
Where other boys begin you stop.
You let no enemy go by,
And made a stronghold of the sky.
You need no Medals, Crosses, Bars:
Your name is written on the stars.

July 19, 1942